COMBAT EDITION

HACKS FOR MINECRAFTERS

THE UNOFFICIAL GUIDE TO TIPS AND TRICKS THAT OTHER GUIDES WON'T TEACH YOU

MEGAN MILLER

SKY PONY PRESS

Sky Pony Press
New York

Sky Pony Press books may be purchased in bulk at special discounts for sales promotion, corporate
gifts, fund-raising, or educational purposes. Special editions can also be created to specifications.
For details, contact the Special Sales Department, Sky Pony Press, 307 West 36th Street, 11th Floor,
New York, NY 10018 or info@skyhorsepublishing.com.

Sky Pony® is a registered trademark of Skyhorse Publishing, Inc.®, a Delaware corporation.

Minecraft® is a registered trademark of Notch Development AB.
The Minecraft game is copyright © Mojang AB.

Visit our website at www.skyponypress.com.

10 9 8 7 6 5 4 3 2 1

Manufactured in China
This product conforms to CPSIA 2008

Library of Congress Cataloging-in-Publication Data is available on file.

Cover photo credit Megan Miller
Book design by Sara Kitchen

Print ISBN: 978-1-51073-804-1
Ebook ISBN: 978-1-5107-4389-2

TABLE OF CONTENTS

INTRODUCTION

If you are new to the game, fighting the mobs in Minecraft can be a bit scary. But once you get used to the mobs and fighting them (and get used to occasionally dying!), it can be a lot of fun. I was not much of a fighter at first, but now I stay up sometimes at night (Minecraft night) just to find and kill some skellies, zombies, and Creepers. It's also a great way to get more experience points so you can enchant more weapons, armor, and tools.

This book has all the information you need to improve your fighting skills against the different mobs in Minecraft, from Blazes to zombie pigmen, and some tips to help you in PvP, as well. You'll learn more about your weapons, and how to enchant them and use potions. The mob profile pages examine each hostile mob: where you'll find it, how to kill it, and what experience points and drops it will give you. On each page you'll also find the number of strikes needed to kill a mob, and these are generally the minimum number of strikes needed. However, you may need fewer strikes if you use the critical hit tactic and more if the opponent wears armor, heals quickly, or if you don't have a fully charged bow.

As with pretty much everything, practice makes perfect. So to become a truly great fighter, get your sword and bow out and start taking out those mobs.

Note: The tips in this book are for the Minecraft Java Edition (PC) 1.12. If you are using a different version of Minecraft, some effects and behaviors may be slightly different. You can research any topic further by visiting the official Minecraft community wiki at Minecraft.gamepedia.com.

CHAPTER 1
SWORDS

Your primary Minecraft combat weapons are, of course, your sword, your shield, and your bow. Your sword is for close combat, or melee, your shield protects you from incoming attacks, and your bow is for distance attacks. However, if you are caught unprepared—while harvesting a crop of melons, for example—you can use a tool if you have one; a pickaxe, axe, or shovel will deal more damage than your bare hands. There are other items in Minecraft you can use and build to inflict damage. Flint and steel and a bucket of lava are two popular warfare weapons.

The wooden sword is your first weapon, unless you are lucky and can get to stone quickly with your wooden pickaxe! One of your first goals in Survival mode should be to upgrade to a stone sword. Then continue upgrading until you have a couple of trusty enchanted diamond swords at your side. Hold your sword in one hand and your shield in the other to attack and block at the same time.

Crafting a Sword

You'll need two blocks of a single type of weapons material (wood planks, stone, gold ingot, iron ingot, or diamond ore) and one stick to make a sword. If you are making a wooden sword, you need to use the same kind of wood for both wood planks and the stick.

Sword recipe: 2 sword material + 1 stick.

You can also acquire weapons from killed mobs and from trading with villagers. Sometimes a zombie will spawn with a sword in hand or a skeleton may spawn with a bow. There's a chance they will drop the weapons when they die, and then they're yours.

Sword Damage

The amount of damage a sword can do depends on the material it is made of. Wooden and golden swords deal the least damage (4 points), stone deals 5 points, iron 6, and diamond 7 points. You can increase the amount of damage you deal by using a critical hit, which you perform by jumping and then striking as you fall. A critical hit increases the damage by up to another 50 percent. Your sword also has a special "sweep" attack. As long as you aren't running, your sword will strike not just your target, but also knock back any other nearby entities and inflict a point of damage. There's a Sweeping Edge enchantment that will increase the sweep attack damage significantly. The drawback to this: You can damage other passive mobs or friendly players too. So make sure Fido is out of the way before you do a sweep!

The Attack Cooldown Phase

After you strike with any melee weapon, it goes through a cooldown phase. During this phase, the weapon will inflict quite a bit less damage. The full recharging phase only lasts a second or so, depending on the weapon, but this can make a big difference in how many blows it takes to smite your enemy.

The length of the attack cooldown phase is decided by a weapon's "attack speed." There are lots of statistics on the phases of the different weapons. You can find these on the official Minecraft Wiki at minecraft.gamepedia.com. However, the easiest way to know when your weapon is fully recharged is to turn on your attack indicator icon. You can do this under Video Settings. You can also choose whether the indicator appears near your crosshair or by your hotbar.

The crosshair attack indicator. Both attack indicators "empty" after you strike and show the level of recharge of your weapon.

Hotbar attack indicator.

Sword Durability

Each weapon—and tool—has a limit on its use called its durability. Durability is measured in number of uses. By far the most durable swords are the diamond swords, which can last for more than 1,500 uses. Only your hands can last longer! Meanwhile, gold is not very durable at all and only lasts 33 uses. Once you've used a weapon the maximum number of times, it breaks and disappears. Here are the stats:

Sword Material	Uses
Wooden Sword	60
Stone Sword	132
Iron Sword	251
Golden Sword	33
Diamond Sword	1562

About Durability

Durability is how long a weapon or tool will last—how many chops, stabs, and swings at an item, mob, or player before it breaks. For example, an iron axe has a durability of 251, which means you can use it 251 times. When a weapon or tool breaks, it makes a clanking sound and disappears from your inventory. If you use a tool or weapon on an item it isn't meant for, like using a sword to break a dirt block, it usually counts as two uses rather than one. So it's good to use the right tool for the job, unless you are in a pickle.

You can quickly see how much you've used a weapon by looking at it in your inventory. At the bottom of the weapon's icon is the durability bar. The durability bar only shows up after you've used the weapon or tool for the first time, and it starts as a full green bar. As you use the weapon, the bar shortens and eventually turns red. Finally, the colored bar disappears, leaving an empty gray space when you are at the end of the weapon's lifetime. However, you still have a couple of uses when the colored bar disappears. The number of uses remaining depends on the material. A gold weapon will have only 2 more uses while a diamond will have 61.

Under the sword, pickaxe, and bow you can see the durability bar.

You can also find out the exact durability remaining on any weapon in your inventory by turning durability tool tips on. To do this, press the F3 and H buttons at the same time. On a Mac, you may need to press the Fn, F3, and H buttons at the same time.

You can see exact durability in item tool tips if you press F3+H to turn this on.

CHAPTER 2
BOW AND ARROW

A bow and arrow is essential for killing mobs from a distance. If you have a chance to kill a mob from a little ways away, take it. This keeps you safe. However, you will still need to get up close to any dropped experience orbs to get the XP points.

Crafting a Bow and an Arrow

The hard part of bows and arrows is getting the resources to make enough of them, especially when you are at the start of your game. You will need three pieces of string, which you get fairly easily from killing spiders with your sword. In the daytime, big spiders are passive, and you can often find a couple spiders in the morning that spawned overnight around your house. They'll turn hostile when you strike your first blow, but at least you start out with the advantage.

Craft a bow with 3 sticks + 3 string.

For arrows, you *can* gather some already made arrows by killing skeletons. Skeletons will randomly drop 0–2 arrows. However, unless you have a skeleton mob farm, you won't get enough arrows from killing skeletons alone. To make your own arrows, you need sticks, flint, and feathers. A flint, 1 stick, and 1 feather make 4 arrows. Ideally, you'll want to have between a half stack and a stack of arrows (32–64) on you pretty much all the time, depending on how often you use your bow. For 64 arrows, you'll need 16 pieces of flint and 16 feathers. And *that* means you'll need to shovel about 160 blocks of gravel and kill about 16 chickens. (You probably will want the Infinity enchantment for your bow as soon as possible! The Infinity enchantment gives you infinite arrows, as long as you keep one single arrow in your inventory.)

Craft arrows from 1 flint + 1 stick + 1 feather.

You can recover some arrows you have shot that missed their marks and landed in the ground or trees, but these won't be enough to keep you supplied. You can't recover any arrows shot by a skeleton or arrows shot while using the Infinity enchantment.

Tipped Arrows

Increase the effectiveness of your attack using tipped arrows. These are arrows crafted with a lingering potion to deliver any potion's status effect to a target. Status effects delivered include Luck, Bad Luck, Strength, Weakness, Invisibility, Night Vision, Water breathing, and seven others. Craft up to eight at a time by placing the arrows around the lingering potion in the crafting table. Spectral arrows, crafted by combining glowstone with up to 8 arrows, make your opponent glow when hit, increasing their visibility at night and when they are hiding.

Bow Durability and Damage

An unenchanted bow will last for 385 uses.

Depending on the strength of your shot (how far you pull the bow back), a bow will cause 1–10 points of damage. You can achieve a critical hit with a bow by pulling it back all the way; this is also called a fully charged bow. The bow will shake a little when fully charged, and the arrow you release will leave a trail of tiny stars. A fully charged arrow can fly as far as 65 blocks. It will give 9 points of damage or, very occasionally, 10.

A fully charged arrow leaves a trail of stars.

Each mob and player in Minecraft has a specified number of health points. Players have 20 health points, and these are represented in your heads-up display (HUD) as hearts. (Your HUD is the set of bars, stats, and inventory hotbar at the bottom of your screen.) As of the 1.9 update, your status effects are also visible in the heads-up display instead of in your inventory. A tiny slime block only has 1 point (half a heart) while the Wither boss has 300 points (150 hearts). Once a mob or player has no health points left, they die. When you strike a mob or player, the tool or weapon you use deals a specific amount of damage points. Each damage point takes away 1 health point. In addition to weapons and tools, things that can cause damage to a mob or player include fire, lava, lightning, cactus, TNT explosions, drowning, falling, suffocating, poison, starvation, the Thorns enchantment on another player's armor, the Wither effect, and just being in the Void. The Void is the empty space beyond bedrock. The land of The End is also surrounded by the Void.

Your HUD shows your health status, hunger status, and experience level above your inventory hotbar.

Repairing Weapons
- - - - - - - - - - - - - - - - - -

You can repair weapons (or armor) by combining a used item with an identical new or used item on your crafting grid. It doesn't matter in which square of the crafting grid you place the two weapons. However, both weapons must be of the same material. Therefore, you can't combine a stone sword with a diamond one. The resulting weapon has the usage points of both weapons added together. If this totaled durability is less than the maximum durability a new version of the weapon would have, you also get a bonus of up to 5 percent of the total possible durability. To get the most benefit from that 5 percent bonus, repair two worn weapons whose added durability is 95 percent or less than full durability for the weapon. If you don't want to check points and do calculations, all you really have to do is make sure to repair weapons whose green bars look like they total up to a bit less than a full green bar. Be careful not to repair an enchanted weapon on the grid. Doing this will remove the enchantments. To repair an enchanted weapon (or tool), you should use an anvil. If you discover the treasure enchantment Mending, you can enchant a favorite weapon to use XP (experience points) as you earn them whenever you are holding the weapon. See the chapter on enchanted weapons for more information.

Repair two used weapons to get bonus durability.

CHAPTER 3

OTHER WEAPONS

You aren't limited to the standard bow and sword for defeating your foes. You can use an interesting variety of other Minecraft items to damage or kill your enemies. Some are excellent substitutes for your sword or bow.

Tools

Axes, pickaxes, and shovels can deal more damage than your bare fists. Like swords, the weakest and least durable tools are made of wood, and the strongest and most damaging are made of diamond. However, they aren't as durable in combat as they are at their assigned task. If you use a tool rather than a weapon to strike a mob, it will count as two uses in durability, rather than one. While some tools may do more damage than a sword, it will take longer to recover from a hit and strike again. Here's a breakdown of how much damage they can do:

	Wood	Stone	Iron	Gold	Diamond
Axe Damage	7	9	9	7	9
Pickaxe Damage	2	3	4	2	5
Shovel Damage	2.5	3.5	4.5	2.5	5.5
Durability (Pickaxe, Axe, Shovel)	60	132	251	33	1562

Using a hoe is the same as using your hands. It doesn't do any more damage and doesn't register any durability hits if it isn't used to till dirt. In some cases, an axe may be a better weapon than a sword. An axe can do more damage than a sword with one hit, but the recovery time is longer. Axes also have a crushing blow attack, where hitting a player's shield can disable it for five seconds, leaving the player open to attack.

Bucket of Lava

A bucket of lava can be a great weapon. You do have to be careful about placing the lava, so you aren't damaged as well. It's best to hop up on a quickly placed block of gravel first. Buckets of lava are best poured at the last minute, so that the enemy is close by or doesn't have enough time to react. In the Overworld, lava will flow 3 blocks away from the block you pour it on. It will also burn most items in its path as well as any mob, except in the Nether. Nether mobs are not damaged by either lava or fire. Lava flows faster in the Nether than in the Overworld.

Flint and Steel

Flint and steel is a small tool crafted from an iron ingot and flint (you get flint from shoveling gravel). You place it on a block and right-click it to set it alight. You can use it against mobs by simply clicking the ground under their feet or the blocks in front of them if they are running. You can make a Creeper explode almost immediately by clicking it with flint and steel. Flint and steel has a durability of 65.

Anvil

Anvils are used primarily for repairing and enchanting weapons and armor. However, they have an interesting characteristic that makes them suitable as weapons. They respond to gravity, and if they are dropped from a good height, they will land with a force powerful enough to kill a mob or player. Anvils will cause approximately 2 points of damage per block fallen, up to a maximum of 40 points (20 hearts).

Anvil Traps: For a very simple anvil trap, you can place an anvil on top of a pillar of signs. This will get the anvil up high enough so that it will cause damage when it falls. At the bottom of the pillar, you need to create a way that a mob or player will break the block that the pillar stands on. When they do this, all the signs will drop, and so will the anvil. You must press Shift when you click to place signs (and the anvil) on top of each other like this. You also need to disguise the pillar of signs if you are trying this on other players in a PvP server. For example, the pillar could be just above a block of diamond in a fake mining corridor that you know players will travel down. Any player mining the diamond block from beneath will be hit. As an even simpler alternative, wait on top of a cliff or roof. Place the anvil in the same way you place gravel when you want it to fall—against another block. The anvil will drop heavily to the ground, injuring any player or mob in its way.

Cutaway of a simple anvil trap.

TNT

TNT is an explosive block in Minecraft. It will kill mobs or players close to it. You can find TNT at the bottom of desert temples or craft it from gunpowder (a drop from Creepers) and sand. To set it alight, you use flint and steel. This gives you a few seconds to run before it explodes. TNT can also be ignited with a flaming arrow, lava and fire, traveling over an activator rail in a minecart, a redstone pulse, dispensers, and more. TNT will destroy up to three-quarters of the blocks around it, unless it's in water. In water it won't destroy anything, but it will give an explosive sound. Two popular combat uses for TNT are TNT traps and TNT cannons.

TNT Trap: To make a TNT trap, place the TNT where you want it. Connect TNT to a trigger mechanism, like a pressure plate or a lever. A player or mob stepping on the pressure plate will start the TNT countdown. Or use a lever to ignite the TNT yourself.

Connect a pressure plate to TNT with redstone. You will want to hide the redstone trail, though!

Arrow Dispenser Trap

An automatic arrow dispenser is another common weapon used in a variety of creative ways in Minecraft. For a simple one that dispenses one arrow at a time, use redstone to connect a dispenser to a pressure plate. The pressure plate should be a short distance away from but right in front of the dispenser's mouth. There is an example on the following page. Once you have it working, you can cover up the redstone with other blocks to hide it. This is something you could place in a corridor in your home to deter intruders!

Simple arrow dispenser.

CHAPTER 4

SHIELDS

Shields are an essential tool for defending yourself in combat. You hold a shield in one hand and a sword in another to switch between blocking and attacking. Since weapons need time to recharge after each hit, it's nice to have a shield so you never have to be completely defenseless.

To use your shield, hold it in either hand and right-click to block almost anything that comes at you, like a mob attack, a creeper explosion, arrows, fireballs, snowballs, and other projectiles. When you use your shield, you will slow down to a sneaking pace. Your shield will absorb the damage from the attack, and a melee attack may knock you back as well. An axe attack may disable the shield for five seconds, leaving you vulnerable, so be sure to have a weapon ready in your other hand to strike back. Blocking an attack with a shield will cause arrows to bounce off.

Modifications

Crafting a shield requires six wood planks and an iron ingot. You can decorate your shield by combining it with a banner crafted from six wool and a stick. You can mend a shield by combining two damaged shields. Mending a shield will remove any banners but add an extra 5 percent durability on top of the combined durability of the two shields. You can also apply Mending and Unbreaking enchantments using the anvil and enchanted books.

CHAPTER 5

ARMOR

rmor is essential in combat. While you can survive occasional attacks from lesser mobs without it, it is armor that lets you survive big damage attacks and continue fighting. Armor protects you from sword or contact attacks from mobs and other players, as well as from arrows, fire, lava, fishing rods, Ghast or Blaze fire balls, fire charges, cactus damage, and explosions. It doesn't protect you from drowning, suffocating, falling, status effects, extended fire exposure, the Void, or Potions of Harming.

Crafting armor requires 24 pieces of the same material, either leather, gold, iron, or diamond. You can't craft chainmail armor, but you can trade villagers for it. Rarely, a skeleton or zombie wearing chainmail armor will drop it when killed.

Full suit of chainmail armor.

Each piece of armor provides 1–8 defense points. Each defense point gives a reduction of 4 percent on incoming damage. On your HUD, you can see the total number of defense points your current armor will provide. A chestplate icon is equal to 2 defense points. The separate armor pieces don't protect specific parts of your body, they just add up total defense points. So if you are just starting out and are very poor on materials, you can start with leather boots or a leather helmet. The boots cost 4 leather, whereas it costs 5 leather for the helmet. They both give 1 point of defense, but the boots will last longer. From the charts below, you can work out which pieces of armor you can afford and what will give you the most protection and last the longest.

Protection from Full Sets of Armor

Material	Full Set Protection
Leather	🛡🛡🛡🛡
Golden	🛡🛡🛡🛡🛡🛡
Chain	🛡🛡🛡🛡🛡🛡
Iron	🛡🛡🛡🛡🛡🛡🛡🛡
Diamond	🛡🛡🛡🛡🛡🛡🛡🛡🛡🛡

Individual Armor Defense Points

	Leather	Gold	Chainmail	Iron	Diamond
Helmet	1	2	2	2	3
Chestplate	3	5	5	6	8
Leggings	2	3	4	5	6
Boots	1	1	1	2	3

Durability

Armor durability is lowered by weapon or melee attacks, explosions, lava, and fire. The greatest damage done to your armor is by TNT explosions or Creeper explosions, but you can halve the durability hit by blocking with your shield. Each attack counts as 1 hit, and 1 point will be taken from the durability of each separate piece of armor. Once the durability of armor reaches 0, the bar disappears and you can use it one more time. Also, if you are using armor that reduces damage, the armor will reduce in durability when you take (and it repels) damage.

	Leather	Gold	Chainmail or Iron	Diamond
Helmet	56	78	166	364
Chestplate	81	113	241	529
Leggings	76	106	226	496
Boots	66	92	196	430

With Minecraft 1.8, you can place your armor on armor stands.

Horse Armor

Horse armor can be found in dungeon, temple, mineshaft, End city, and stronghold chests as well as in village blacksmith shops. There are three types of horse armor. Iron armor gives the horse 20 percent protection, gold gives 28 percent, and diamond 44 percent. Although you can't enchant it, horse armor has unlimited durability, so you don't have to repair it.

Horse with diamond armor.

CHAPTER 6

ENCHANTING

Enchanting and brewing potions aren't easy to do at the beginning of the game. Usually these activities will have to wait until you've gathered the proper resources. However, getting to this level should be a major goal if you want to survive well in Normal or Hard mode. Enchanted weapons and armor make a huge difference in surviving combat, as can potions. They are absolutely necessary for fighting the strongest mobs, like the Ender Dragon and Wither.

Enchanting comes before brewing potions, because you don't have to go to the Nether to start enchanting. To start enchanting, you need an enchantment table, which you craft from obsidian, books, and diamonds, and lapis lazuli to pay for the enchantments. The levels of enchantment you can give to an item are increased by surrounding the table with up to 15 bookshelves. There are different levels for enchantments. For example, a Protection IV enchantment will give more protection than a Protection I enchantment.

Crafting an enchantment table.

To enchant, click on the enchanting table and place the item you want to enchant in the left slot. In the right panel, you'll be given three choices of enchantment. It will tell you how many experience levels you need to perform the enchantment, as well as how much lapis lazuli (and how many experience levels) it will cost. Select the enchantment you want on the right and then remove your enchanted item. Sometimes you will get additional enchantments with the one you picked. Enchanted items have a magical glow.

In the enchanting screen, you can mouse over the three enchanting options for a tooltip that shows what one of the enchantments will be.

The higher your experience level (shown in your green experience bar), the more XP points you need to get to the next level. Because the best enchantments require level 30, you should stop and enchant something whenever you get to level 30. Going from level 27 back to level 30 is faster than going from level 30 to 33.

Armor Enchantments

The **Protection** enchantment reduces any kind of damage. **Fire Protection** reduces damage from fire, and **Blast Protection** reduces damage from explosions. **Projectile Protection** protects you from damage from arrows and Ghast or Blaze fireballs. **Feather Falling** (boots only) reduces damage from falls. **Depth Strider** (boots only) allows you to move more quickly in water. **Respiration** (helmet only) helps you breathe and see under water. **Aqua Affinity** (helmet only) makes it easier to mine underwater. **Thorns** inflicts a small amount of damage on anyone attacking you. Of all these, Protection is often the best, because it gives you general protection from almost everything. However, once you start getting lots of diamonds, you can think about creating different suits for armor for different occasions: visiting the Nether, fighting guardians, or caving.

Enchanted armor can help you move, breathe, and mine underwater.

Sword Enchantments

Sharpness increases damage. **Smite** increases damage more, but only to undead mobs, and **Bane of Arthropods** does the same for spiders, silverfish, and Endermites. **Fire Aspect** will light your target on fire, and **Knockback** will knock him, her, or it back. **Looting** gives a chance of getting better drops from your hostile mobs. Of all these, choose Sharpness over Smite and Bane of Arthropods. Looting is also very helpful for getting those rare drops. The Sweeping Edge enchantment will add more damage to your sweep attacks.

Bow Enchantments

Power increases damage, while **Punch** gives more knockback. **Flame** will send a flaming arrow to deal fire damage. **Infinity** means you need only a single arrow in your inventory to shoot as much as you want. Of all these, choose Infinity if you have any issues with arrow making, and then Power.

Treasure Enchantments

Some enchantments can only be found as treasure in chests, or by fishing, or in trades with villagers. Frost Walker enchants armored boots to freeze water as you walk across it. Frost Walker I freezes a one-block radius around you, where the higher numbers create more ice with each step. It's a great way to cross water without a boat. The ice isn't permanent, however, so stride quickly before it melts!

The Mending enchantment fixes your favorite weapons by using the XP you earn as you use them. Fighting a hostile mob with your favorite sword? For every XP orb you get, your sword will regain some durability. Keep an eye out for the Curse of Binding enchantment, which means you can't remove an item enchanted with this until you die or the item breaks. The Curse of Vanishing means that if you die, the cursed item will disappear forever.

Using Gold

It might seem from all the stats that gold is a waste of time as a weapons or tool material. It has terrible durability, and a golden sword doesn't do more damage than the lowly wooden sword. However, gold has a special attribute that you should keep in mind. It is more "enchantable"—you can get better enchantments for the same XP cost as another material. That means you are more likely to get Sharpness IV at your enchanting table with a golden sword than a diamond sword.

Repairing Enchanted Weapons

Anvils allow you to repair an enchanted weapon and keep its enchantments. You do this by placing your worn item on the left and either a new item of the same material on the right or, in some cases, the material the item is made of, like diamond or iron. You can also combine two enchanted weapons of the same material to combine enchantments. An anvil also allows you to combine an unenchanted weapon with an enchanted book to place the book's enchantment on the weapon. If you combine two similar items with the same enchantment level, the resulting item will be given the next level enchantment, if there is a next level. For example, you can combine two Sharpness IV swords to make a Sharpness V sword.

Repairing with the anvil will also cost experience levels; here it is just one level.

CHAPTER 7

POTIONS

Potions will help you in battle tremendously. They can restore your health, make you invisible, or make you faster and stronger. They are a must when you are fighting boss mobs like the Wither. You will be ready to start making potions when you start visiting the Nether and killing the mobs there, as they supply much of what you need. For example, to make a brewing stand, you'll need a Blaze rod dropped by a Blaze. When you have drunk a potion, a notice shows up on your inventory screen along with how long the potion will last, if it isn't an instant potion.

Brewing

First, fire up your brewing stand with blaze powder. Next, place up to three bottles of water and add a base ingredient—usually Nether wart—to create a "base" potion called the Awkward potion. Then brew your base potion with a new ingredient to make a primary potion, which will give the drinker a special status effect, like Speed, for a certain amount of time. One chunk of blaze powder can be used on twenty ingredients before it needs to be replaced. You can create a hopper to automatically dispense blaze powder as it's needed so you don't need to refill it as often.

Brewing the Awkward Potion with Nether wart and water.

Then, if you want, you can brew your primary potion again with a modifying ingredient to create a secondary potion. Use glowstone to make the effect stronger, or gunpowder to make it into a splash potion. Finally, you can add dragon's breath to turn any splash potion into a lingering potion, which creates a cloud effect.

Brewing the Potion of Regeneration with a Ghast tear and the Awkward Potion base.

Modifying the Potion of Regeneration by brewing it with gunpowder to make a splash potion.

Dragon's Breath

When fighting the Ender dragon, if you can keep your wits about you long enough, have an empty bottle ready. The dragon's breath attack emits a purple cloud that you can collect in a bottle and apply to any splash potion to create a lingering potion. This is a great feature when you want to disable a group of hostile mobs, help your allies, or create multiple tipped arrows at one time.

Weaponized Potions

With a splash potion, you can use the potion as a weapon. The splash potion looks a little like a grenade, with a pin at the top. Splash potions are much more effective when they are thrown at the hitbox of the mob or player, rather than an adjacent block, like the block the mob is standing on. Think of the hitbox as an invisible box around an entity or item that defines where it can be struck or clicked on. Be careful of using potions on the undead, though. On skeletons, zombies, and the like, splash potions can work in reverse. A Potion of Harming will heal a skeleton, a Potion of Healing will harm it, and a Potion of Regeneration won't have any effect. The undead, spiders, and the Ender Dragon also won't be affected by poisonous potions.

Basic Potions and Ingredients

Awkward (Base Potion)	Water and Nether Wart
Fire Resistance	Magma Cream
Healing	Glistering Melon
Leaping	Rabbit's Foot
Night Vision	Golden Carrot
Poison	Spider Eye
Regeneration	Ghast Tear
Strength	Blaze Powder
Swiftness	Sugar
Water Breathing	Pufferfish
Harming	Potion of Water Breathing or Poison + Fermented Spider Eye
Slowness	Potion of Swiftness + Fermented Spider Eye
Weakness	Doesn't Use Awkward Potion as a Base, Just Water with Fermented Spider Eye

CHAPTER 8

FIGHTING TECHNIQUES

...n improve your combat skills by practicing sc...
...iques. Certain techniques work better for spec...
...n others.

...You can prevent up to 100 percent of damage...
...strike by using a shield. When using a shield...
...sneaking pace.

Right-click with
shield to block d
from incoming a

Block-Hitting: You will not be able to block with your shield and strike with your weapon at the same time. While it may be tempting to click continuously as you attack, block with your shield after each strike to let your weapon recharge to inflict maximum damage. However, when you block you are moving slower, so this tactic is best used when you don't anticipate having to run around. Also, if your opponent can't see you, they can't hit you, so there's no need to block-hit when you are behind someone, for example.

Knockback: To knock-back an opponent, sprint to them and hit them while sprinting. This can knock a player back almost twice as far as regular hit. The only mobs you don't want to use this against are skeletons (this can give them time to recharge their bows) and any mob that you have difficulty catching.

Encircling: Circle around your enemy. This makes it harder for them to hit you. If you can keep behind the other player or mob, you can deliver damage while they can't.

Critical Hits: When you are falling through the air, you deliver up to 50 percent more damage to foes. Jump, and as you fall, strike. You can practice these as you slaughter your herd of cows or pigs.

Jump, then strike as you fall for a critical hit, which will show stars around your foe.

Strafing: If your enemy is using a bow or other projectiles, use your A and D keys to move left and right as you approach your enemy to make it harder for them to hit you.

Sword Timing: Check your sword timing. As you begin an attack, the attack strength of your weapon goes down with each hit. Weapons cool down and recharge at different rates. You can change the video settings on your game so that an attack strength meter shows up every time you begin an attack. Turning on the meter will help you time your clicks to make every strike count. Let the meter fill up as high as possible before striking again, especially against powerful Nether mobs.

Aiming: When you aim with your bow (or with any projectile), take into account the direction your opponent is moving. If they are moving to your right, aim a little right, so they walk into your arrow. If you are waiting for an opponent to come into view, prepare by charging your bow, and keeping it extended, until they appear and you can shoot a critical arrow hit, practically before they even notice you. If you are fighting up close and using your arrow, you may not have time to fully charge your bow. Charge it halfway by pulling for a couple counts and then shooting and recharging.

Arrows fall as they fly, so aim above your target. Practice will help make you perfect.

Stunning with Fishing Rods: Many Minecraft PvP warriors like to use fishing rods in combat. Right-clicking your opponent as you run toward or away from them stuns them for a moment, allowing you more time to attack them or to escape.

Hide Surprise Weapons: If you are about to use flint and steel, or a bucket of lava, don't hold it until the last minute. When you hold it, your opponent will see it in your hands and know what you are about to do. This can give them a chance to escape. Use the number keys on top of your keyboard, 1–9, to switch quickly between weapons.

Ender Pearl Escape: You can use Ender Pearls to teleport anywhere you can aim the Pearl. It will damage you slightly, but much less than a fall from a height, a fall into lava, or a melee in which you are outgunned or outnumbered.

Water Fighting: If you can get your opponent into water, that will slow them down. If you are both in water, get below them. Your reach is longer from this angle than from the position above, so you can avoid their swings while still hitting them.

Keep Eating: Your hunger level is the most important thing in making sure you heal quickly. Make sure you have plenty of good food, like steaks or baked potatoes, to eat when your hunger drops.

Practice: Set up a world where your only goal is to fight, die, and fight again. If you turn cheats on, you can use Creative mode to gather armor, food, weapons, and more into chests. That way, when you switch to Hard mode, you won't have to spend time roasting that cow and can concentrate on fighting.

CHAPTER 9

THE MOBS YOU FIGHT

The word *mob* is short for mobile. Mobile was used in early multiple-player gaming to describe any entity that could move.

Mob Types

In Minecraft, mobs can be classed in several ways, like how aggressive they are or where they spawn.

Passive mobs will never attack you; these include bat, chicken, cow, donkey, horse, mooshroom, mule, ocelot, parrot, baby polar bear, pig, rabbit, sheep, skeleton horse, squid, and villager.

Neutral mobs are passive except in certain circumstances, when they become hostile. Neutral mobs are the cave spider (at high light levels), Enderman, iron golem, llama, adult polar bear, spider (at high light levels), wolf, and zombie pigman.

Hostile mobs attack you without being provoked. They include the Blaze, baby zombie, chicken jockey, Creeper, Elder Guardian, Endermite, Ghast, Guardian, Illagers (Evoker, Vindicator, vex), magma cube, shulker, silverfish, skeleton (and variants, like the Stray), slime, spider jockey, witch, Wither, Wither skeleton, zombie (and variants, like the Husk), and zombie villager.

Darkness mobs spawn in low light levels in the Overworld. Darkness mobs include the Enderman, skeleton, Creeper, spider, and zombie.

The Darkness mobs come out at night.

Nether mobs spawn only in the Nether. Nether mobs include the Ghast, magma cube, and zombie pigman.

Local mobs spawn in specific areas in the Overworld or Nether. Overworld local mobs are cave spiders, slimes, silverfish, and witches. Nether local mobs are Wither skeletons and Blazes.

Utility mobs are mobs that were created to serve. Iron and snow golems are utility mobs. Iron golems can spawn naturally in large villages, and protect villagers by attacking hostile mobs. Snow golems can only be created by the player, and they also attack most mobs.

Iron and snow golems can help you out in a pinch.

Boss mobs have a more complicated programming than other types of mobs and are able to heal themselves. They have very high levels of health and attack strengths, so they are difficult to kill. Boss mobs include the Ender Dragon and the Wither.

Hostile Mob Behavior

Hostile mobs spawn within 24–128 blocks of a player. Most can see any player that is within 16 blocks of them; some can see further. When a mob sees the player in its line of sight (there are no opaque blocks in the way), it begins to pursue the player. If a hostile mob is 128 blocks away from a player, it will despawn or disappear. However, if you put a nametag on a mob, it won't despawn. Some hostile mobs can spawn with or pick up weapons and armor, and if they have these, they also won't despawn.

Once they spawn, they walk around randomly. However, if there is no player nearby (within 32 blocks), they'll stop walking after about 5 seconds and just stand still.

Almost all mobs are vulnerable to the same things players are: drowning, lava, suffocation, cactus, TNT explosions, and fall damage. Mobs are also damaged by fire, except for Nether mobs, who live in the fiery biome of Hell and are used to such things.

Almost all mobs are vulnerable to the same kinds of damage players are. These Creepers have been caught in lava.

CHAPTER 10

BABY ZOMBIES AND CHICKEN JOCKEYS

Baby Zombies

Baby zombies are miniature zombies. There are baby versions of zombies, zombie villagers, and zombie pigmen, and they all behave pretty much exactly the same way. About 5 percent of zombies spawn as baby zombies. The drops the babies give are the same as for their adult version. They can be equipped and pick up armor or weapons like the adults.

A baby zombie villager and a baby zombie pigman.

Chicken Jockeys

A chicken jockey is a baby zombie, baby zombie villager, or baby zombie pigman riding a chicken. They are very rare. There is a 5 percent chance that a baby zombie will spawn as a chicken jockey. This works out to a 0.25 percent chance for a chicken jockey to spawn. That's means about 1 in every 400 zombies will be a chicken jockey. However, if there are chickens nearby when the baby zombie spawns, its chance of becoming a chicken jockey are almost doubled.

A chicken jockey.

Baby zombies and chicken jockeys may be cute, but they're harder to fight than the slow adults. They are very fast!

If the baby's riding a chicken, you can't kill it by pushing it over a cliff. The chicken can just flutter slowly down to the ground without it or its rider being harmed. If a chicken jockey comes into contact with flowing water, it separates into the baby zombie and the chicken.

BABY ZOMBIE STATS

Mob Type: Hostile, Darkness

Health: Chicken – 4 ♥♥

Baby Zombie – 20 ♥♥♥♥♥♥♥♥♥♥

Attack Strength:

Easy – 2 ♥

Normal – 3 ♥♥

Hard – 4 ♥♥

Experience: 12

Drops: Rotten flesh, 1 raw chicken, 0–2 feathers, more rarely 1 carrot, 1 potato, any armor or weapons it holds, 1 iron ingot, or 1 gold ingot (for a baby zombie pigman)

Spawn: Baby zombies and chicken jockeys spawn in the Overworld at light level 7 or below. Baby zombie pigmen spawn in the Nether.

Sword Strikes to Kill (Baby Zombie):

Wood: 4

Stone: 4

Iron: 3

Gold: 4

Diamond: 3

Bow Strikes to Kill: 3

Fighting a Baby Zombie or Chicken Jockey

To fight these kids, you will need to use your sword, because they run so fast. They are pretty hilarious, but if you don't pay attention they can still kill you. They can also run through 1x1-block gaps. The best way to defeat a chicken jockey or baby zombie, once it has set its mark on you, is to attack as fast as you can. If you can, get two straight blocks above the baby zombie (by pillaring with two blocks of gravel, for example) and strike it from there.

CHAPTER II

BLAZE

Blazes are hostile mobs found in Nether fortresses. They have a body made of dark gray smoke surrounded by three sections of four whirling golden rods. They are fierce opponents. Once they see you, they fly up in the air, catch on fire for a moment, and then rapidly hurl three fire charges at you. They'll repeat these actions over and over again. While it might seem best to avoid blazes entirely, they drop blaze rods, which are essential for several Minecraft activities. You need one blaze rod to make a brewing station for potion, and blaze powder powers a potion stand and makes the Potion of Fire Resistance. You also need blaze powder to make Eyes of Ender, which you are required to find and repair the End portal.

Blazes can spawn randomly in Nether fortresses, but you will also find special rooms in a fortress that house blaze spawners. These rooms are up a short flight of stairs and have short walls topped by Nether fence.

A Blaze spawner in a Nether fortress.

BLAZE STATS

Mob type: Hostile, Nether, Local

Health: 20 ❤❤❤❤❤❤❤❤❤❤

Attack Strength (Fire Charges): 5 ❤❤❤

Attack Strength (From Contact):

   Easy – 4 🖤🖤

   Normal – 6 🖤🖤🖤

   Hard – 9 🖤🖤🖤🖤🖤

Experience: 10

Drops: 0–1 Blaze rods (in console edition may drop 0–2 glowstone dust)

Spawn: In Nether fortresses randomly or through a Blaze spawner, at low light levels (11 or less)

Sword Strikes to Kill:

 Wood: 4, but don't bother if you don't have armor and strong swords. Unless you're on Easy, you'll be quickly overpowered and killed by fire damage, both from the fire charges and from contact by the blazes.

 Stone: 4

 Iron: 4

 Gold: 4

 Diamond: 3

Fighting the Blaze

The blaze is one of the more difficult mobs to fight. It flies up and down and back and forth, often out of reach. It fires its charges at you very quickly, and when it is on fire itself, it will give you significant fire damage when it touches you. A fire resistance potion will protect you greatly from the blaze. However, to make potions, you first need a blaze rod to create a brewing station. So if you have not killed any blazes yet, you will not be able to make potions. In this case, you can use an enchanted golden apple, which gives you several status effects for a short time, including Absorption, Regeneration, Resistance, and five minutes of Fire Resistance.

After hurling its charges, the blaze needs a few seconds to recharge.

Surprisingly, snowballs are a pretty good tactic to use against blazes. They deliver three points of damage to the blaze. A common tactic is to throw snowballs at the blaze initially, and then run in with your sword to kill it. If you have Fire Resistance from a potion, you can also try hooking it with a fishing rod to bring it close and then attack with your sword. Blazes are also damaged by water, but water sizzles and disappears in the Nether.

Once a blaze spawns, you have a few seconds while it gets ready to deliver the fire charges. After it hurls the charges (which it will only do if you are in its line of sight and within 16 blocks), it will take another few seconds to recharge. Use these moments to deliver as much damage as you can. If you can hide behind a block, you can pop out to draw the blaze's fire, hide again to dodge the charges, then come back out to attack during the short lull. However, this is much harder to do when you have multiple blazes bearing down on you!

You can also create a space whereby you are below the blaze, protected by blocks such as Nether brick, with just a one block gap that allows you to strike the blaze with your sword. If another mob, like a Wither skeleton, is nearby, hide behind it. If you are lucky, the blaze will hit the skeleton, which will then attack the blaze. Once they are engaged, you can attack the blaze yourself.

CHAPTER 12

CAVE SPIDER

Like their larger cousin, the spider, the cave spider is a neutral mob in light levels of 9 and above, and hostile at lower levels. It looks just like a regular spider, but it has a bluish fur and is smaller and faster. It is also poisonous on Normal and Hard difficulty levels. However, they don't spawn naturally like other mobs, they only spawn from spawners found in abandoned mineshafts. You can identify a cave spider spawner by the masses of cobwebs surrounding it. These mob spawners themselves look like a cage the size of a block with a miniature mob spinning around inside. Cave spiders, like spiders, can climb blocks vertically, like climbing a ladder.

Cave spiders are smaller than the regular spider, taking up less than a full 1x1 block of space. This means they can fit through a space as small as a block wide and a half block tall. Because of their small size and speed, they can be difficult to defeat.

CAVE SPIDER STATS

Mob Type: Neutral, Local

Health: 12 pts ❤❤❤❤❤❤

Attack strength:

Easy – 2 ❤

Normal – 2 (with venom) ❤

Hard – 3 (with venom) ❤◖

Experience: 5 pts

Drops: 0–2 string, 0–1 spider eye

Spawn: Spawn in abandoned mineshafts only, at low light levels

Sword Strikes to Kill:

Wood: 3

Stone: 2

Iron: 2

Gold: 3

Diamond: 2

Bow Strikes to Kill: 2

Fighting the Cave Spider

To defeat the cave spider, you need to kill existing and spawning spiders and disable or destroy the spawner itself. Because they are so fast, you will be using a sword against them instead of the bow, which takes several moments to pull and charge before you can fire an arrow.

You will find yourself trying to battle these spiders at the same time as trying to destroy enough cobwebs around the spawner so that you can disable it. You can use a bucket of water to remove cobwebs, and shears are the fastest tool to cut them. Water will also uproot any torches placed on the ground, so be aware of where your torches are. One tactic is to close off the ends of the corridor they are in, and then tunnel in just above or below the spawner, so you can quickly destroy it with your pickaxe or place torches on each side. Placing torches will create enough light that it prevents spiders from spawning, disabling it.

Try to avoid letting these spiders get above you, where they can jump on you and damage you. The venom from their bite will cause you enough damage to bring you down to a half-heart of health. It won't kill you, but it will leave you very vulnerable to dying from anything else. Once you are bitten, retreat and use potions or milk to heal before you strike again. If you don't care about losing the spawner or any drops and experience points, you can pour a bucket of lava on it.

CHAPTER 13

CREEPER

eepers are one of the four main hostile mobs you encoun-
er in the Overworld. The other three are skeletons, spiders,
zombies. Creepers are mottled green, have four tiny rect-
lar legs, and spawn in low light levels. Unlike zombies and
tons, they don't die in the sunlight—although we all wish
would.

biggest problem with Creepers is their silence. You can
a zombie's groans and the scritching sound of a spider, but
pers are very nearly silent. If you are lucky, you may hear a
rustle. But unless you are facing toward them as they ap-
ch, the last thing you will hear is the sizzle of a fuse burning
re the Creeper explodes a block away from you, taking you
n with it.

If the Creeper has been hit by lightning, it becomes the even deadlier charged Creeper. A charged Creeper has a bluish tinge flowing around it to signify the electric charge. Its explosion causes more damage than a TNT explosion.

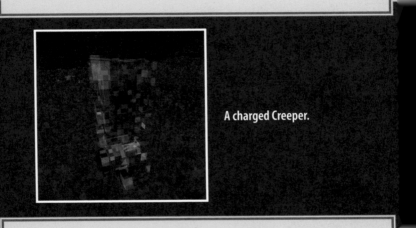

A charged Creeper.

Once either type of Creeper spots you (you have to be within 16 blocks), it will chase you. If you are wearing a creeper head, however, it will only recognize you when it gets within 8 blocks. When it is within a block of you, it will start to sizzle and swell. And once it starts to sizzle, it will explode in 1.5 seconds. If you get away from it (about 3–5 blocks, depending on your difficulty level) within 1 second, the Creeper will not explode.

A swelling Creeper on the left and an exploding Creeper on the right.

CREEPER STATS

Mob Type: Hostile, Darkness

Health: 20 ♥♥♥♥♥♥♥♥♥♥

Attack Strength (Maximum):

Normal – 49 ♥♥♥♥♥♥♥♥♥♥
♥♥♥♥♥♥♥♥♥♥
♥♥♥♥♥

Charged – 97 ♥♥♥♥♥♥♥♥♥♥
♥♥♥♥♥♥♥♥♥♥
♥♥♥♥♥♥♥♥♥♥
♥♥♥♥♥♥♥♥♥♥
♥♥♥♥♥♥♥♥♥♥

Drops: 0–2 gunpowder, a music disc (if killed by a skeleton), and a Creeper head (if killed by a charged Creeper).

Spawn: In the Overworld at light levels of 7 and below.

Sword Strikes to Kill:

Wood: 4

Stone: 4

Iron: 4

Gold: 4

Diamond: 3

Bow Strikes to Kill: 3

The best way to kill a Creeper is with your bow and arrow, keeping well away from it. If you can't do this, sprint straight to the Creeper and strike it with your sword. Striking it while you sprint will knock it back more than if you don't sprint. The moment you hit the Creeper, press S to move backward immediately. It is better to move backward after you've knocked the Creeper back, rather than try to angle left or right. If you move forward, you will still be too close to it. You can also do this maneuver without sprinting, but the timing is more critical. In either case, repeat the swoop in, smack back, and swoop out procedure until the Creeper dies. You may want to practice ahead of time switching quickly from the W key to move forward and the S key to move back.

As with most mob killing, the best sword enchantment for Creeper killing is Sharpness and the best bow enchantment is Power. If you can add knock back via the Knockback (sword) or Punch (bow) enchantment, that is also a big help, especially for the swoop in and out tactic.

CHAPTER 14

ELDER GUARDIAN

The Elder Guardian (a larger, more powerful version of the Guardian) is an ocean-dwelling hostile mob that appears with a new ocean monument structure. There are three Elder Guardians spawned with each ocean monument, and they will not respawn if you kill them. They live inside the monument. One is in a top room near the monument's treasure (8 gold blocks, hidden by prismarine blocks); the other two live in rooms on opposite wings of the monument.

You can find the rare ocean monument in deep ocean.

The Elder Guardian is very similar to the Guardian; it attacks in the same way, by laser and its defensive spines, but it deals more damage. It gives the same drops with one additional possibility, the dry sponge. Also like the Guardian, it swims suddenly and quickly and attacks both players and squid. Guardians will swim away from an approaching player to gain some range for its laser beam. However, the Elder Guardian has the unique ability to inflict players within a 50-block radius with Mining Fatigue III for five minutes. This is a status effect that will really slow down your mining, making it very difficult to break blocks. When the mob inflicts you with this, you'll see a shadowy image of the Elder Guardian on your screen for a moment.

ELDER GUARDIAN STATS

Mob Type: Hostile, Local

Health: 80 ♥♥♥♥♥♥♥♥♥♥♥♥♥♥
♥♥♥♥♥♥♥♥♥♥♥♥

Attack Strength:

> Easy – 5
>
> Normal – 8
>
> Hard – 12
>
> When Being Attacked – 2

Experience: 10

Drops: 0–1 raw fish, 0–2 prismarine shards, 0–1 prismarine crystals, 1 wet sponge; it will also drop raw salmon, clownfish, or pufferfish.

Spawn: Spawns only at an ocean monument, and only once with each ocean monument. Unlike other hostile mobs, they don't despawn, except in Peaceful level.

Sword Strikes to Kill:

Wood: 16

Stone: 14

Iron: 12

Gold: 16

Diamond: 10

Bow Strikes to Kill: 9

Fighting the Elder Guardian

As with fighting the Guardian, you will need to prepare your armor and potions for fighting and moving underwater: Aqua Affinity, Respiration, and Depth Strider enchantments, and Potions of Swiftness, Night Vision, and Water Breathing. You can also use Potion of Invisibility to prevent the Guardians from seeing and attacking you; this is a good tactic.

The Elder Guardian will inflict you with mining fatigue to prevent you from mining to find the hidden blocks of gold.

Like fighting the Guardian, your best move is to attack quickly and attack hard with your sharpest enchanted sword. Because of the Mining Fatigue, you likely won't be able to mine to find the gold blocks hidden in the middle of the monument, so your first goal is to take out the three Elder Guardians.

CHAPTER 15

ENDER DRAGON

The Ender Dragon is a large, black dragon with reddish purple eyes. It is the largest mob in the game, over 20 blocks long. There is only one Ender Dragon, and it is found in the End, a world you travel to through the End portal. After defeating the dragon the first time, you can summon it to return by placing one End crystal on either side of the End portal.

The End is a series of islands made of a special block called End stone, and tall columns of obsidian rise from the ground. The island island is surrounded at a distance by an infinite number of small islands, floating in an endless dark space called the Void. If you fall off the edges of the islands and into the Void, you will die. The Ender Dragon lives on the central island, and you must defeat it in order to visit the outer islands. It flies among the tops of several obsidian columns that have special blocks of crystals on top of them. These crystals regenerate the dragon's health when it is injured, making it very difficult to slay the dragon.

When the Ender Dragon is close to you, its purple health bar appears at the top of your screen. When it attacks you, the Ender Dragon flies right at you. It destroys all blocks besides obsidian and End stone in its path and causes damage to you when it hits you, as well as knocks you back. It may fly off for a little while, but will return to attack you again.

ENDER DRAGON STATS

Mob Type: Boss

Health: 200

Attack Strength:

Easy – 6

Normal – 10

Hard – 15

Breath attack – 6

Fireball attack – 12

Experience: 12,000

Drops: Dragon egg

Spawn: Only once, in the End, but can be regenerated by the player

Sword Strikes to Kill:

Wood: 40 (These Strikes to Kill stats are purely theoretical. Because of the way the Ender Dragon heals itself and flies quickly, you will need an enchanted diamond sword and enchanted bow to kill the dragon, and you may strike many more times than this in the game, because you will miss often.)

Stone: 34

Iron: 29

⚔ Gold: 40

⚔ Diamond: 25

🪶 **Bow Strikes to Kill:** 23

Fighting the Ender Dragon

Before you go to the End, you must be prepared. First, you want to make the portal room safe and place chests to hold extra supplies. Then place a bed and sleep there to reset your spawn point. That way, if you die without killing the Dragon, you can enter the End again quickly with new supplies.

For supplies, you will need enchanted diamond armor, diamond swords, tipped arrows, and enchanted bows. Plan on bringing an extra set of armor, three swords, and three bows. Because you will be fighting for a long time, you need several stacks of tipped arrows or the Infinity enchantment on the bow. You will also want to bring at least a stack of obsidian to create a bridge from your spawn point to the main island and safe platforms. In addition to plenty of food, other supplies to consider are empty bottles to capture dragon's breath, the makings for an army of iron and snow golems, and potions of Healing and Regeneration.

To fight the Ender Dragon, you must first destroy its healing crystals, which are on top of obsidian pillars. They look like cubes rotating in fire. A few are protected by iron bars: you'll have to climb up to destroy the bars. You can also tell a crystal is present when a damaged dragon flies by one and the crystal emits a ray to heal it. To destroy the crystal, you can throw any projectile at it, even projectiles that don't do damage. You can use your bow and arrow or throw snowballs or eggs. If you hit the crystal, it explodes with more force than TNT, so you don't want to be close! You may want to climb other obsidian pillars and make a safe ledge area using obsidian to fire on other crystals.

These crystals heal the Dragon, making it very difficult to kill. You'll have to destroy these first.

You will also have to deal with hordes of Endermen wandering around. You don't want to provoke them by looking at them, but it's easy to make a mistake. To prevent them from seeing you look at them, you can wear a pumpkin as a helmet. However, this also limits your ability to see well. To keep them occupied, you can unleash armies of iron and snow golems who will attack Endermen automatically and distract them.

Once you've destroyed all of the healing crystals, it is time to take on the Ender Dragon. The best weapon to use is the bow. Wait until the dragon is heading for you, and shoot for its head. Shooting the dragon's head causes full damage. If you shoot it anywhere else, you will only give the dragon about a quarter of the damage from your bow. You will need to do this over and over again, healing yourself as you get damaged. The Ender Dragon is immune to lava, potions, and fire. You can only damage the Ender Dragon with explosions or your sword or bow. Arrows will bounce off a sitting dragon without causing any damage, so plan your attacks when the dragon is in the air. You also have a short window of time to attack the dragon with your sword when it perches for a few seconds on the center, empty portal. When it perches, it is immune to arrows.

When you finally kill the dragon, it explodes with impressive flashing rays. Its death creates an End exit portal for you to travel back to the Overworld, as well as a dragon egg. The dragon egg doesn't do anything itself. If you click it, it will teleport several blocks away, so it is very difficult to gather. (Hint: If you can get it to drop on a torch, it will turn into a collectible item.)

Since the dragon is the boss mob of Minecraft, defeating it the first time will cue credits, signaling you have "won"; however, your battling days are far from over. You can respawn and beat the dragon as many times as you want! The first twenty times, a new End portal will appear that can teleport you to an outer island where you can battle shulkers and collect rare loot.

Getting to the End

The End is a dark land, like the Nether, populated only by Endermen and the Ender Dragon. To get there, you must first find a portal, which is in a stronghold. Strongholds are complex mazes of dungeon-like rooms, corridors, and stairways, and there are only three in the Overworld. You'll find prison cells, libraries, and fountain rooms in a stronghold. To find a stronghold, you first gather fifteen or so Ender Pearls by killing Endermen. You craft these into Eyes of Ender using Blaze powder. (You can also trade with villagers for Eyes of Ender.) When you throw an Eye of Ender into the air, it will move in the direction of the nearest stronghold and then drop back to the ground. Pick up the Eye and travel in the direction it pointed. Every so often, throw another Eye into the sky to check your direction. When you are directly over the stronghold, the Eye you throw will fall and sink down into the ground. Now you dig! Once you reach the brick walls of the stronghold, you must break through and find the portal room, which has a silverfish spawner and a broken portal in it. The portal has places for Eyes of Ender to go in 12 frames along its border, but many are missing. You place your Eyes of Ender in the frames to fix the portal. Then you can jump in to travel to the End. Be prepared—the first time you visit the End you can return to the Overworld only by dying or killing the Dragon.

CHAPTER 16

ENDERMAN

Endermen are 3-block-tall black mobs with very long arms and legs. They wander about the Overworld and the End in their own little clouds of purple stars and occasionally pick up a block and hold it. (They're the reason your Minecraft neighborhood has all those little one-block holes in the ground!) They are neutral unless you provoke them, which happens by merely looking at them anywhere from their upper legs to their head. Moving the crosshair over these parts is considered looking, so it's not terribly difficult to avoid them, at least in the Overworld. You can look at their legs without a problem. There are so many Endermen in the End that avoiding looking at them is much more difficult.

ENDERMAN STATS

Mob Type: Neutral, Darkness

Health: 40

Attack Strength:

Easy – 4 🖤🖤

Normal – 7 🖤🖤🖤🖤

Hard – 10 🖤🖤🖤🖤🖤

Experience: 5

Drops: 0–1 Ender Pearls, used to make Eyes of Ender

Spawn: In light levels of 7 and less in the Overworld, the Nether, and the End.

Sword Strikes to Kill:

Wood: 8

Stone: 7

Iron: 6

Gold: 8

Diamond: 5

Bow Strikes to Kill: 5

Fighting the Enderman

When you provoke an Enderman by looking at it or by attacking it, it will shudder and shake and make a very unsettling and long groan, like a disturbed airplane. It will teleport toward you suddenly and damage you by contact. When you attack it and it receives damage, it will teleport away and then back to you again, often behind you.

You can't use a bow, other projectiles, or a splash Potion of Harming on an Enderman, as it will teleport away before contact is made.

However, the Enderman has several weaknesses that you can use to your advantage.

- It can't pass under gaps less than three blocks high.
- Usually it doesn't teleport if you attack its lower legs.
- Contact with water causes damage.
- It becomes neutralized by damage from rain, lava, or sunlight.

If you are on the hunt for Ender Pearls and need to kill Endermen, make a little outpost with a 2-block high, 2-block deep gap you can fit into. Stare at an Enderman and nip into your outpost, keeping your back at the wall. When it teleports to you, attack only its legs with your sword. You'll get very little damage, if any, and quite possibly an Ender Pearl out of the deal.

You can defeat Endermen pretty easily by staying in a 2-block high gap and striking their feet.

You can also pillar 3 blocks up, stare at an Enderman, and strike it with your sword when it teleports close by. It can't teleport to your block or fly, so you can swing at it at your leisure. However, it's harder to swing just at its legs, so it may teleport away, leaving you Ender Pearl free.

CHAPTER 17

ENDERMITE

The Endermite is a new mob that came in the Minecraft 1.8 Bountiful Update. Its body is based a little on the silverfish. They look like tail-less, chubby, purple silverfish and, like the silverfish, they are low in health and attack damage. They can also jump up a block like silverfish, suffocate on soul sand, and make similar death squeals. They only spawn rarely, when you use an Ender Pearl or when an Enderman teleports away.

ENDERMITE STATS

Mob Type: Hostile

Health: 8 ♥♥♥♥

Attack Strength: 2 ♥

Experience: 3

Drops: None

Spawn: There is a 5 percent chance that an Endermite will spawn when you throw an Ender Pearl. They can also spawn when an Enderman teleports away.

Sword Strikes to Kill:

 Wood: 2

Stone: 2

Iron: 2

Gold: 2

Diamond: 1

Bow Strikes to Kill: 1

Fighting the Endermite

You can fight the Endermite with your sword at close quarters without having too much harm done to you. A few sword strikes will do it in, and it won't call any pals to help it out. However, they despawn after only a few minutes.

CHAPTER 18

GHAST

The Ghast is one of the largest mobs in Minecraft and has 9 long, hanging tentacles. They float in the sky of the Nether, and if they see you and you are close enough, they will open their mouths to emit a fireball aimed right at you.

GHAST STATS

Mob Type: Hostile, Nether

Health: 10 ❤❤❤❤❤

Attack Strength:

Easy – 9 ❤❤❤❤❤

Normal – 17 ❤❤❤❤❤❤❤❤❤

Hard – 25 ❤❤❤❤❤❤❤❤❤❤❤❤❤

Explosion: Depends on distance

Experience: 5

Drops: 0–2 gunpowder, 0–1 Ghast tears

Spawn: In the Nether.

Sword Strikes to Kill:

Wood: 2

Stone: 2

Iron: 2

Gold: 2

Diamond: 2

Bow Strikes to Kill: 1–2

Fighting the Ghast

The Ghast can shoot from a very long range—up to 100 blocks—but it won't shoot its fireballs at you unless it has line of sight to you. The fireballs aren't very fast, so you have some time to hide, if that's what you want to do.

Otherwise, fire up your bow, as that is the easiest way to kill a Ghast. They don't usually come too close. To protect yourself, you can build a cobblestone or obsidian wall to nip behind. As the Ghast fires at you, the fireballs will catch Netherrack near you on fire, and this is almost as dangerous. If you can create a cobblestone area to fight from, this can help. If the Ghast is far away, make sure to aim high.

You can also bounce its fireball right back at the Ghast. The fireball travels slowly, so you have enough time to punch it back with your bow or your shield. You can even use your fist and not be damaged or shoot an arrow at the fireball. If you aim the punch just right, you can send the fireball right back to the Ghast, killing it *and* getting the achievement Return to Sender.

A Ghast opens its eyes and mouth right before firing.

It is difficult to get the Ghast drop, a Ghast tear. This is used to make the very handy Potion of Regeneration. Typically, the Ghast will be flying over lava when your arrow hits it, and its drops will land in the lava and burn up. One solution is to hook the Ghast with your fishing rod, draw it toward you, and then attack it with your sword once it is over land. Use a sword enchanted with Looting to maximize your plunder.

CHAPTER 19

GUARDIAN

The Guardian is a brand new mob introduced with the Minecraft 1.8 Bountiful Update. It and the Elder Guardian are the only two hostile mobs of the sea. Guardians spawn nearby a new structure called the ocean monument. An ocean monument is similar to the desert temple and jungle temple, although there are no chests inside. There is a central treasure room in the ocean monument, where 8 gold blocks are hidden behind dark prismarine blocks.

GUARDIAN STATS

Mob Type: Hostile, Local

Health: 30 ♥♥♥♥♥♥♥♥♥♥♥♥♥♥♥

Attack Strength:

Easy – 4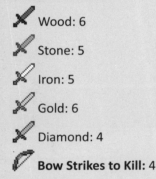

Normal – 6

Hard – 9

Experience: 10

Drops: 1–2 raw fish, 0–2 prismarine shards, 0–1 prismarine crystals.

Spawn: In the ocean by ocean monuments.

Sword Strikes to Kill:

Wood: 6

Stone: 5

Iron: 5

Gold: 6

Diamond: 4

Bow Strikes to Kill: 4

Fighting the Guardian

Because you'll be fighting underwater, you will need to prepare armor and potions that will help you breathe, see, and move quickly beneath the ocean surface.

The Guardian swims suddenly and quickly in and around its ocean monument, attacking players and squid. It attacks by

g its laser at you. However, first it must charge its l
e this is happening, the laser is purple and does no dam
n, when it is fully charged, the beam turns yellow, del
low, and stops. A few seconds pass before the Guardiar
arge. The laser can reach about 15 blocks to hit you, as
here are no solid blocks between the Guardian and yo
tion, if you attack the Guardian while its spikes are or
deal you 2 points of damage.

Guardians zap you with rays to damage you.

aring armor and enchanted armor can help protect you
Guardian's laser. It might seem best to stay at a distanc
your bow and arrow. However, arrows don't travel we
water, and the Guardian moves quickly. It can easily da
he way and zap you. Your best tactic is to be aggressiv
. Corner the Guardian so that it can't escape you, and a
uickly with the sharpest sword you have.

CHAPTER 20

ILLAGERS

Illagers are the dastardly, gray-faced cousins of villagers. Luckily, you'll find them only in the rare Woodland Mansion. There are two types of Illager: the Evoker and the Vindicator. Both types are hostile to you, to Iron Golems, and to villagers.

If you get within 12 blocks of an Evoker, it will attack you. First the Evoker raises its arms to summon three companion mobs, Vexes. A Vex is a small, flying illager-like mob. It flies through blocks and strikes at you with its tiny sword. However, a vex will stay close to the location they were summoned in, so it won't follow you forever.

If you get too close to the Evoker, it will summon a fang attack. An offensive fang attack brings 16 iron-like fangs from the ground to snap at you. A defensive fang attack (if you are closer than three blocks) brings two snapping circles of fangs around the evoker. After a few moments, the fangs shrink and disappear.

An Evoker's offensive fang attack brings a fast-moving row of iron teeth out to you.

EVOKER STATS

Mob Type: Hostile, Local

Health: 24

Fang Attack Strength: 6 ♥♥♥

Experience: 10

Drops: 0-1 emeralds, 1 totem of undying

Spawn: Inside Woodland Mansion

VINDICATOR STATS

Mob Type: Hostile, Local

Health: 24 ♥♥♥♥♥♥♥♥♥♥♥♥

Attack Strength:

Easy – 7 ♥♥♥♥

Normal – 13 ♥♥♥♥♥♥♥

Hard – 19 ♥♥♥♥♥♥♥♥♥♥

Experience: 5

Drops: 0-1 emeralds

Spawn: Inside Woodland Mansion

VEX STATS

Mob Type: Hostile, Local

Health: 14 ♥♥♥♥♥♥♥

Attack Strength:

Easy – 5 ♥♥◖

Normal – 9 ♥♥♥♥♥

Hard – 13 ♥♥♥♥♥♥◖

Experience: 3

Drops: 0-1 iron sword

Spawn: Spawned by Evokers

Fighting the Evoker and Vexes

Use a bow (enchanted preferably) as many times as possible to strike the Evoker from further away than 12 blocks, to prevent it from summoning the vexes. If you surprise the Evoker by accident, go after the vexes first with your sword. Then try to get some distance from an Evoker, firstly to stop it from spawning more vexes, and secondly so that you can use your bow.

When the Evoker spots you, it will raise its arms in a magical swirl to summon three flying vexes.

Fighting the Vindicator

A Vindicator will also attack you as soon as you're 12 blocks away. As with the Evoker, it is safest to use a bow to kill it or damage it first. If it's close to you, use a shield to defend yourself and in between blows, strike it back with your own enchanted ax or sword.

If you name a vindicator "Johnny" with a nametag, it will become hostile to all creatures, running from one to the next with its axe raised. Good stuff.

The vindicator raises its axe as it chases you, in an unsettling reminder of a few horror movies.

CHAPTER 21

MAGMA CUBE

Magma cubes are square 2x2 mobs that bounce. They have dark red and black skin and yellow and red eyes. Their accordion-like body expands as they hop up and retracts when they hit the ground.

MAGMA CUBE STATS

Mob Type: Hostile, Nether

Health*:

        Large – 16 pts ♥♥♥♥♥♥♥♥

        Medium – 4 ♥♥

        Tiny – 1 ♥

*Magma cubes also have hidden armor points, which protect them against up to nearly 50 percent of the damage you cause. This means their health, in practice, is higher than the number of hearts they have, and it will take more strikes to kill them.

Attack Strength:

Large – 6

Medium – 4

Tiny – 3

Drops: 0–1 magma cream (only medium and large magma cubes drop these)

Spawn: In the Nether.

Sword Strikes to Kill (Large):

Wood: 4

Stone: 3

Iron: 3

Gold: 4

Diamond: 2

Bow Strikes to Kill: 2

Fighting the Magma Cube

The most difficult thing about fighting mobs in the Nether is your location. There are cliffs of Netherrack with dangerous and life-threatening drops, and lava seas, pools, and dripping columns are everywhere. Half the battle is making sure you are somewhere relatively safe and aren't backing up to a drop into lava. You can increase your chances by using Fire Protection enchantments on your armor and Feather Falling on your boots.

Magma cubes jumping.

Magma cubes are similar to their Overworld cousins, slimes. If you kill a large cube, it spawns 4 medium-sized ones. And when you kill a medium-sized cube, it spawns four tiny cubes. If you are using a diamond sword on a large magma cube, it won't take long to kill. However, if you don't have a diamond sword, an iron sword with Knockback enchantment is a very good alternative. The cube keeps bouncing toward you, and it damages you if it lands on top of you. Knockback helps propel the cube backward so it can't land on you. If it is jumping over you, you still have a chance to stab it with your sword while it is over you. Magma cubes are slow enough that you can take them out with a bow and arrow. The smaller cubes move slowly and have low enough health that it isn't too hard to exterminate them pretty quickly.

CHAPTER 22

SHULKER

In the very purple world of End cities, you'll find a shy yet hostile creature called the shulker. Short for shell lurker, the shulker hides in an armored shell that blends in with surrounding purpur blocks. The shell pops open every now and then to see where you are. But don't let its cute hide-and-seek game fool you. If it sees you're coming too close, it shoots guided projectiles, called bullets, at you that cause you to levitate for ten seconds and then drop to your possible doom.

Destroying all shulkers in a space will leave it clear of the creatures forever, as they do not respawn, but that is easier said than done. Shulkers will teleport away when they are unprotected by adjacent purpur blocks, when they take damage, or when they feel threatened, so they are a tough little mob to pin down and destroy.

SHULKER STATS

Mob Type: Hostile, Local

Health: 30 ♥ x15

Attack Strength: 4 ♥♥

Experience: 5

Drops: None

Spawn: End City

Fighting the Shulker

When its shell is closed, the shulker is immune to arrows, so timing is important. When open, the shell remains open for one to three seconds, leaving the shulker completely vulnerable to attack, so be ready with a charged bow and tipped arrows before it closes again.

The shulker will begin its attack as soon as it sees you are within 16 blocks of its shell. To avoid being hit by a shulker bullet, keep moving. Prepare to fight the shulker with boots enchanted with Feather Falling in case you are hit to avoid damage when the levitation effect wears off.

The shulker is immune to fire and lava. Since you're better off battling the shulker from a distance, a bow and arrows are your best defense. When the shulker's health is less than 50 percent, there is a one in four chance it will teleport away.

You will need to defeat the shulker guarding the End ship treasure, which includes chests with rare loot and the even more rare Elytra.

CHAPTER 23

SILVERFISH

The silverfish lives in strongholds, igloo cellars, woodland mansion "portal" rooms, and in the extreme hills biome. They are invisibly embedded in seemingly normal stone blocks (called monster eggs), and will emerge only if you break their block. It's one of Minecraft's smallest mobs, taking up less space than a block. However, a silverfish can jump 1 block high and can push a player. It will scurry with a wiggling motion straight to you and inflict 1 point of damage when it touches or pushes you. That's not so bad, compared to other hostile mobs. However, if you attack a silverfish directly, with a weapon, other silverfish nearby (within about 10 blocks) may be woken up and come to join the first silverfish in attacking you back. A silverfish can also disappear into another stone block, making it into a monster egg.

Silverfish will suffocate if they are on a patch of soul sand that is too big (around 5x5 blocks or larger) for them to hustle off. If they are on just one block of soul sand, they can usually get off the block before they die.

SILVERFISH STATS

Mob Type: Hostile, Local

Health: 8 ♥♥♥♥

Attack Strength: 1 ♥

Experience: 5

Drops: None

Spawn: From silverfish spawners in strongholds and monster eggs in extreme hills biomes, woodland mansion "portal rooms," and igloos. With a spawner, silverfish can spawn on stone blocks at any light level, but on non-stone blocks only at light level 11 or lower. They can't spawn within 5 blocks of a player.

Sword Strikes to Kill:

🗡 Wood: 2

🗡 Stone: 2

🗡 Iron: 2

🗡 Gold: 2

🗡 Diamond: 1

🏹 **Bow Strikes to Kill:** 1

Fighting the Silverfish

In general, the silverfish's low health and mild attack strength make it easy to kill quickly. If you kill a silverfish in one hit, which you can do with a diamond sword, it won't awaken the other silverfish hiding in monster eggs nearby. You can also enchant a diamond or iron pickaxe with Sharpness, so that it gives 8 or more attack damage, and use that for mining in extreme hills. That way, when a silverfish emerges, you can give it one swing with your pickaxe and continue mining.

One silverfish is easy to kill, but a swarm can overtake you.

If you don't have a diamond sword or enchanted pickaxe, use an indirect way to kill the silverfish, so that it doesn't wake up other silverfish. Jump on a short pillar of gravel (2 high), and drop lava or gravel on it. To suffocate the silverfish with gravel, you do have to place the gravel against a wall or pillar block so that it can slide down directly on top the silverfish. The silverfish gives a nice, long death squeal when you do this! However, because you need to place the gravel carefully so that it suffocates the silverfish, the better solution is a bucket of lava. You can also use flint and steel very handily to set a single silverfish ablaze. It will die without awakening others.

Although one silverfish by itself is not very harmful, a swarm of silverfish can quickly kill you. If you awaken a swarm of silverfish, you will definitely want to pillar up so that they cannot get to you. When you are mining in extreme hills, make sure you have a short stack of gravel on hand and a bucket of lava.

Whatever you do, don't attack the silverfish with a splash potion, especially a splash Potion of Poison. A Potion of Poison makes multiple "attacks," and with each attack, more silverfish are alerted and you could end up with a very large swarm. A Potion of Harming gives an instant effect so you can kill one silverfish with one splash. However, if there are several silverfish present, some may not be killed by the splash and are then able to summon others.

Mining Monster Eggs

Monster eggs can look like any of the stone blocks: cobblestone, stone, stone brick, cracked stone bricks, mossy stone bricks, or chiseled stone. In an extreme hills biome, they'll appear as stone. However, monster eggs take noticeably longer to mine with a pickaxe than a regular stone block. Once you've mined a few, you'll be able to tell while you are striking a stone block if it is a monster egg. (If you use your hands, monster eggs are actually faster to mine than stone.) When you've woken a silverfish from its egg, a little white cloud appears that looks like the cloud that forms when you kill a mob.

CHAPTER 24

SKELETONS AND SKELETON RIDERS

The skelly is one of the big four—the four common mobs of the Minecraft Overworld (the others are the zombie, the spider, and the Creeper) that you'll see daily. When a skeleton is near, you will hear the tinkly sound of bones rattling together.

Although skeletons spawn with a bow, some are able to pick up weapons. If they pick up a more damaging sword, they'll use that instead. Some skeletons spawn with armor or enchanted bows, which will make them harder to kill.

If they are within 16 blocks of you, they will chase you. If you get 16 blocks away from them again, they'll lose interest in you.

Wolves chase and attack skeletons without provocation, and the skeleton will run away when it sees a wolf. They will also now run away from a Creeper that is gearing up to explode.

Strays are a variant of skeleton you'll find in icy biomes. They have a ghostly, blueish look and their arrows will affect you with 30 seconds of Slowness.

SKELETON STATS

Mob Type: Hostile, Darkness

Health: 20 ♥♥♥♥♥♥♥♥♥♥

Attack Strength (Bow):

Easy — up to 4 ♥♥

Normal — up to 4 ♥♥

Hard — up to 5 ♥♥♥

Attack Strength (Sword):

Easy — 2 ♥

Normal — 2 ♥

Hard — 3 ♥♥

Experience: 5

Drops: 0–2 arrows, more rarely bows and armor (which may be enchanted, but usually badly damaged)

Spawn: In Overworld at light levels 7 and below, and by skeleton spawners found in dungeons. Also spawns more rarely in the Nether, near Nether fortresses.

Sword Strikes to Kill:

Wood: 4

Stone: 4

Iron: 3

Gold: 4

Diamond: 3

Bow Strikes to Kill: 2

Fighting the Skeleton

When a skeleton attacks you, it fires its arrows more rapidly the closer it gets. With the knockback of an arrow hit from it, you'll find it is difficult to get close enough to use a sword, and you can be hit multiple times while you're trying to do so. Your best defense is your shield. Raise it up to sneak towards the skelly, and then strike at the skeleton in between its own shots at you. If you don't have a shield, strafe. Use your left and right move keys (A and D) to move left and right. Avoid knocking a skeleton back during a close fight, as this actually gives the skeleton more time to charge and fire its bow.

If you are mining in a cave and you've captured a skeleton's attention, draw it to a location where there are some blocks you can hide behind. When it starts coming around the corner of the block, attack the edge of it before it fully emerges. As with other mob attacks, use the blocking technique to limit the damage the skeleton does.

Skeletons and other mobs are more likely to spawn with armor, weapons, and enchantments in Hard difficulty or when it is a full moon.

Skeletons burn in the daylight, unless they are wearing a helmet or a pumpkin (or are in water), so one passive tactic is to try to draw them out into the open during the day. Once they've taken some damage, finish them off with your sword or bow so you can reap the rewards of dropped loot.

Skeletons are not solid, which leads to an interesting scenario. If you are close to one, and its back is against a wall, walk right up into the block it is standing in. You are now inside the skeleton and can hit it with your sword. Meanwhile, all the skelly can do is fire its arrows meaninglessly into the ground. Score!

Skeleton Riders

Some horses will turn into skeleton riders if you come within 10 blocks and trigger a skeleton trap. The horse will be transformed into a skeleton horse and rider, and three other skeleton pairs will appear nearby. Each one appears with an enchanted helmet and bow, and they fight like skeletons but move very quickly, strafing ahead to attack and backing up when approached. If they spawn in the Nether, there's a good chance the rider will be a wither skeleton. To kill a skeleton rider (also known as a skeleton trap horse), take down the rider with your bow and arrow first before going for the skeleton horse.

CHAPTER 25

SLIME

The slime is a large (2x2x2 blocks) cubed mob. It's green, very slightly transparent, and makes a squelchy sound as it hops straight toward you. When you kill the large slime, it breaks into up to four smaller ones. These split into up to four tiny ones when you kill them.

There are two good things about slimes. One, they're not too fast and not too strong, so they're not difficult to kill. Second, they provide slimeballs as a drop, which you can use to make magma cream, leads to tie animals to posts, sticky pistons, and slime blocks you can bounce on.

Slimes are actually relatively rare. In swamps, they will only spawn at night where the light is 7 or below. The moon also affects when they spawn. They spawn more during a full moon and not at all during a new moon. They can also spawn at any light levels at lower depths of the world (levels 0–39), but only under special conditions and in 1 of about 10 chunks. A chunk is a segment of the Minecraft world that is 16 blocks square and the full height of the world, 256 blocks. Chunks are used in the programming code to manage mobs spawning and despawning and rendering, among other things.

SLIME STATS

Mob Type: Hostile, Local

Health:

Big – 16

Small – 4

Tiny – 1

Attack Strength:

Big – 4 pts

Small – 2 pts

Tiny – 0

Experience:

Big – 4

Small – 2

Tiny – 1

Drops: 0–2 slimeballs, from tiny slime

Spawn: Swamps in low light and in levels below 40.

Sword Strikes to Kill (Big Slime):

Wood: 4

Stone: 3

Iron: 3

Gold: 4

Diamond: 2

Bow Strikes to Kill: 2

Fighting the Slime

Slimes are not very difficult to kill. Use your sword and click fast. Although the smaller slimes will seem like they can overtake you, they are very easy to kill. You can punch a tiny slime with your fist and it will die and give you a slimeball for your effort. Overall, they are mostly just a hindrance, especially if you are mining and come across a slime-generating chunk. When you do, block off your mining corridors to leave just one-block gaps that only the smaller slimes can get through.

Killing a large or medium slime will spawn up to four additional smaller slimes.

CHAPTER 26

SPIDERS AND SPIDER JOCKEYS

You can always tell when a spider is nearby because of its typical scratchy hiss. (If you can hear one but can't see it, it's probably just overhead, in a tree or on your roof.) Spiders are neutral at higher, daylight levels of light. In the dark, at light levels of 7 and below, they become hostile. And once hostile, they never revert back to neutral.

Spiders are very agile, and they can move quickly and jump across a 3- or 4-block gap. They can also climb up vertical blocks, as if the blocks had ladders attached. Spiders are two blocks wide, so they can't fit through 1x1 gaps. They do fit through 1 high x 2 wide spaces, though.

Before the latest 1.9 Combat Update, spiders could not see and track you through walls. With 1.9, they can now find you even if there is a wall between you and the spider.

If you are playing on Hard mode, spiders can sometimes spawn with a status effect. A status effect is a special ability, usually delivered through a potion. Spiders in Hard mode can spawn with Invisibility, Regeneration, Strength, or Swiftness effects that are pretty much permanent.

SPIDER STATS

Type: Neutral (Hostile at low light levels)

Health: 16 ♥♥♥♥♥♥♥♥

Attack strength:

Easy – 2 ♥

Normal – 2 ♥

Hard – 3 ♥♥

Experience: 5

Drops: 0–2 string, 0–1 spider eye

Spawn: In the Overworld, in light levels of 7 or less, and in dungeons from spider spawners.

Sword Strikes to Kill:

Wood: 4

Stone: 3

Iron: 3

Gold: 4

Diamond: 2

Bow Strikes to Kill: 2

Fighting the Spider

Because spiders are fast, the best way to kill them is with a bow and arrow, if you have the chance. If you must use a sword, first try to make sure you are on higher ground than the spider. If the spider is above you, it can jump on top of you and cause extra damage. If you can't get to higher ground, move to a flatter area so that the spider at least isn't above you.

You can also use flint and steel to set a spider alight. Make sure you are a couple blocks away so you don't catch on fire also! For extra power against the spider, enchant your sword with the Bane of Arthropods enchantment, as this will deliver extra damage to spiders. If you are doing well with experience levels and can enchant extra swords, you can enchant one sword to use while mining.

You can also use the width of the spider to your advantage to slip through a 1-block wide gap and attack the spider through the gap. Overall, the spider has lower health than the other four common mobs (zombie, skeleton, and Creeper, which all have 20 points of health), so it is a bit easier to defeat.

Beware the Spider Jockey

Very rarely, a spider will spawn with a skeleton riding on its shoulders. About 1 in 100 spiders spawn this way. This hybrid monster is called a spider jockey and is a deadly combination. It carries all the attack strength of both a spider and skeleton put together. It has the climbing ability of a spider and the accurate aim of the skeleton. However, you will have to kill each one of them separately, and each will provide its separate drops: arrows and bones or string and spider eyes.

Ideally, when you spot a spider jockey, you will run away and hide, so as to preserve your life. If you have enchanted weaponry and armor though, or are confident in your combat skills, you can be bolder. Use your bow and arrow, first to kill the skeleton on top and then the spider.

About 1 in 100 spiders spawn with a skeleton rider.

CHAPTER 27
WITCH

Witches look a lot like villagers, except for their tall black hats, purple cloaks, and grayish skin. Their noses are big like a villager's, but a witch's nose can wiggle and has one large wart on it. Despite their good looks and charm, witches are one of the most harmful mobs you encounter in the Overworld on a normal day. If you are low on health, it might be best to avoid them, as they are difficult to kill and can inflict a lot of damage. They are difficult to kill because they heal themselves while you are fighting them. They use helpful potions on themselves and throw harmful potions at you.

When witches were first introduced in the game, they only spawned in witch huts. Witch huts are small wooden homes raised above the water in swamps. A witch still spawns with a witch hut, but they can also spawn anywhere in the Overworld where there is a light level 7 or below, so you may find one in your spelunking expeditions. And if a villager is struck by lightning, it turns into a witch.

WITCH STATS

Mob Type: Hostile, Local

Health: 26 ♥♥♥♥♥♥♥♥♥♥♥♥♥

Attack Strength: Witches attack you through potions, and two will cause damage to your health (the Potion of Poison and Potion of Harming). One potion of poison can cause up 38 or more points of damage but will always leave you with 1 point of health, so it won't kill you. A Potion of Harming can cause up to 12 points of health.

Experience: 5

Drops: 0–6 sticks, 0–6 gunpowder, 0–6 sugar, 0–6 spider eyes, 0–6 glowstone dust, 0–6 redstone, 0–6 glass bottles, (more rarely) 1 potion (Healing, Fire Resistance, Swiftness, or Water Breathing)

Spawn: In the Overworld at light levels 7 or less and witch huts in the Swamp biome. Villagers who are struck by lightning will turn into witches.

Sword Strikes to Kill:

 Wood: 6

Stone: 5

⚔ Iron: 4

⚔ Gold: 6

⚔ Diamond: 4

🏹 **Bow Strikes to Kill:** 3

Fighting the Witch

There is a logic to what potions witches will throw at you and when. When you are within 8 blocks of a witch, it will throw a Potion of Slowness at you to slow you down, unless you already are under a Slowness status effect. If you don't retreat, and your health is 8 points or over, they'll throw a Potion of Poison at you. Poison won't kill you, but it can take you down to a single point of health (half a heart). Then, if you get within 3 blocks of a witch, they sometimes throw a Potion of Weakness, as long as you aren't already inflicted with a Weakness effect. Finally, once you have been inflicted by Slowness and Poison, they'll start throwing Potions of Harming. These can and will kill you.

Meanwhile, as soon as the witch sees you, the witch drinks potions to heal itself. They'll guzzle a Potion of Healing when they're damaged and a Potion of Fire Resistance if they're on fire. If they're underwater, they can drink a Potion of Water Breathing. Also, if they are 12 or so blocks away from you, they can drink a Potion of Swiftness so they can quickly get close to you before they attack.

This witch has just drunk a Potion of Healing and thrown a Potion of Slowness.

The best way to fight a witch is to use your bow and arrow from a distance. The bow has a longer range than a witch throwing splash potions, so you can come out of the battle completely unscathed. If long range is not an option, your best bet is to rush the witch immediately. If you can, surprise them by keeping hidden as long as possible. Get in as many strikes with your sword as you can before they start drinking their Potion of Healing. (You can tell they're drinking their potion by the bubbles floating up from them.) You can kill a witch quickly with fast swordplay before they even get around to throwing the Potion of Harming.

When you do kill them, they'll drop materials from potion making, sometimes a stick (perhaps from their unseen broomstick?) and, more rarely, a potion that they were about to drink.

CHAPTER 28

THE WITHER

The Wither is an extremely powerful boss mob. It is the only hostile mob in the Minecraft game that the player creates. To create a Wither, you must have been to the Nether to collect soul sand and three wither skeleton skulls. You arrange the soul sand blocks in a T-shape and then place the skulls on the top three blocks. When the last skull is placed, the blocks turn into the Wither boss mob. You must place one skull as the last block or the Wither won't spawn.

The spawning of the Wither is a dramatic event. The sky turns slightly darker, and the Wither flashes blue. It grows larger and larger, gaining health. (Like the other boss mob, the Ender Dragon, the Wither's health bar will show on your screen.) During this period, it is immune to any attacks. Finally, when its full health is reached, the Wither flashes and creates a giant explosion around itself and changes into its final, somewhat larger form. A black, flying, skeleton-like, three-headed, projectile-hurling hostile form. The Wither immediately and constantly attacks any living entities it sees—you, a cow, everything—flying from target to target. The projectiles it hurls are Wither skulls. There are two types of Wither skull it can throw: fast black ones and slower, rarer blue skulls. Both have the same explosive power as Ghast fireballs. The black skulls can't explode hard blocks like cobblestone, while the blue skulls can break all blocks except for bedrock and the End portal frame. So the Wither causes a lot of destruction—to the world around you and to you.

THE WITHER STATS

Mob Type: Boss

Health: 300 x 15

Armor Points: 4

Attack Strength:

Easy – 5

Normal – 8

Hard – 12

(On Normal and Hard, the Wither attack also gives Wither effect, which is similar to poison.)

Experience: 50

Drops: 1 Nether star

Spawn: Initiated by player.

Sword Strikes to Kill:

 Wood: 60

Stone: 50

Iron: 43

Gold: 60

Diamond: 38

Bow Strikes to Kill: 34

Fighting the Wither

There are quite a few reasons not to create and fight the Wither. (1) The Wither has 100 more points of health than the Ender Dragon. (2) It can throw three Wither skulls at a time, some of which can destroy any blocks except bedrock. (3) Besides blast damage, Wither skulls also inflict the Wither effect on you. This drains your health and also makes it difficult to see what your health is because it turns your health bar black. (4) Inflicting the Wither effect on you actually heals the Wither by 5 points. (5) It is immune to fire and lava. (6) If you get the Wither down to half health, it suddenly gets Wither armor protection, which makes it immune to arrows. (It can't fly at this point, which is a plus.) (7) The only potion you can use against a Wither is the Potion of Healing, as it is an undead mob.

There are two reasons to fight the Wither yourself: (1) for the bragging rights and (2) for the ultra rare drop, a single Nether star. Killing the Wither is the only way to get a Nether star, and a Nether star is the key ingredient for creating beacons. Beacons are made of glass, Nether star, and obsidian. In addition to making a powerful light beam, if you place a beacon on a pyramid of iron, diamond, emerald, or gold, you can give yourself and anyone nearby the beacon special status effect powers.

To take on the Wither, you must have enchanted armor and weapons. You won't survive without it, and you'll pretty likely die even with it. You can make it much easier on yourself if you go to the End and defeat the Ender Dragon first. Then you can go back to the End to stage your Wither battle there. In the End, the Wither will also attack Endermen, who will join in the fight. They will help you get the Wither to half health, when at least it can't fly any more.

Regardless, you will want to stage your battle away from your home base, to protect it from the massive explosive destruction that will be caused. Enlist any help you can, from other players on multiplayer servers or by building iron golems. Use obsidian to create a safe area, and to protect the extra armor, weapons, and potions you will need. If possible, create a special space, walled with obsidian, to confine your battle and reduce unnecessary amounts of flying about and chasing.

The Wither firing an explosive skull at you.

Your bow should be enchanted with the highest Power and Punch level you can afford, as well as Infinity. Your sword, also, should be enchanted with the highest Smite level, along with Knockback. (Looting won't help deliver more Nether stars.) In addition, brew multiple bottles of Potion of Healing, both for yourself and to harm the Wither, along with several Golden Apples, and some Potions of Strength, Regeneration, and Swiftness. For your armor, get the highest level of Blast Protection, if you can. Before your battle, eat an enchanted apple and drink your Strength, Swiftness, and Regen potions. Use your bow for the first half of the battle, then when the Wither is no longer flying, use your sword. Good luck!

CHAPTER 29

WITHER SKELETON

Wither skeletons look similar to regular Overworld skeletons, but they are 2.5 blocks high instead of 2. Their bones are a dark grayish black. They only spawn in the Nether, in or by Nether fortresses. The mouth of a Wither skeleton is not as wide as a regular skeleton. Whereas skeletons are equipped with a bow, the Wither skeleton carries a stone sword. Like skeletons, Wither skeletons will run away from wolves and can pick up armor and weapons. Unlike Overworld skeletons, they won't burn in daylight. They will flash with fire for a moment, but they aren't killed or damaged. They aren't damaged at all by either lava or fire, because they are natives of the Hell biome of the Nether.

Wither skeletons strike you with their sword, which gives you the Wither effect, similar to poisoning. The Wither effect lasts

10 seconds and gives 1 point of damage every couple of seconds. When you've received the Wither effect, your health bar turns black. You can heal yourself with milk, potions, and the like. Wither skeleton attacks will knock you back, so be especially careful if you are near cliffs or ledges.

WITHER SKELETON STATS

Mob Type: Hostile, Nether, Local

Health: 20 ♥♥♥♥♥♥♥♥♥♥

Attack Strength:

> Easy – 5 ♥♥♥
> Normal – 8 ♥♥♥♥
> Hard – 12 ♥♥♥♥♥♥

Experience: 5

Drops: 0–1 coal, 0–2 bones, (more rarely) a stone sword or 1 Wither skeleton skull, used to create a Wither boss.

Spawn: In or near Nether fortresses at light level 7 or lower.

Sword Strikes to Kill:

 Wood: 4

Stone: 4

Iron: 3

Gold: 4

Diamond: 3

Wither skeletons move fast. They walk as fast as a player and also can sprint. And because they can deal a fairly large amount of damage to you, it is best to be prepared and plan safe places or escape routes, especially if you are visiting the Nether without powerfully enchanted weapons and armor. For example, because Wither skeletons can't pass through 2-high blocks, you can place blocks on fortress corridor ceilings to prevent them from following you. Have Potions of Healing or Regeneration at the ready.

First, at a distance (12 blocks or so), use a bow enchanted with Power as well as Punch. Punch will knock back the target, which can buy you some more time. Closer to the skeleton, use your sword. Once you are close, though, it is highly likely that this mob will give you the Wither effect. You'll want to keep a melee as short as possible, so use a diamond sword enchanted with Sharpness or Smite. The Smite enchantment is even more damaging to undead mobs than the Sharpness enchantment, so if you can spare an extra sword to use just against the undead, do so. (However, you'll often find Blazes and Wither skeletons nearby or together, and the Smite enchantment doesn't work against blazes.)

That said, the most powerful enchantment for damaging your enemy is Smite V or Sharpness V. A diamond sword with either of these will kill a Wither skeleton in one strike. With Smite IV or with Sharpness IV, you'll need just two strokes to kill it. Because Wither skeleton skulls are rare and essential for creating a Wither, try to use a Looting enchanted sword to improve your chances of getting a skull.

u can't kill the Wither skeleton in one stroke, retreat
e a 2-high block that it can't enter. Draw it near you, a
your sword, then quickly move back into your safe
of range of their sword. Heal if you need to, and repea

A Wither skeleton standing next to its cousin, the regular skeleton.

CHAPTER 30

WOLF

A wolf can exist in three states: wild, tamed, and hostile. A wild wolf is grayish and its tail droops down. A hostile wolf has red eyes and makes snarling or growling sounds. A tamed wolf has lighter fur, its tail angles up, and it has a collar.

Wild wolves are neutral and won't attack you. They live in small groups, or packs, and attack sheep and rabbits. All wolves, including tame ones, will also attack skeletons without being attacked first by them. However, if you attack a wild wolf, all wild wolves nearby will turn hostile and attack you. They will continue to be hostile and attack you until you die. A tamed wolf never becomes hostile to players.

WOLF STATS

Mob Type: Neutral

Health:

Wild – 8

Tame – 20

Attack Strength (Wild):

Easy – 3

Normal – 4

Hard – 6

Attack Strength (Tamed): 4

Experience: 1–3

Drops: None

Spawn: In Forest and Taiga biomes.

Sword Strikes to Kill (Wild):

Wood: 2

Stone: 2

Iron: 2

Gold: 2

Diamond: 1

Bow Strikes to Kill (Wild): 1

A hostile wolf's tail sticks straight out and it has red eyes, an unprovoked wild wolf's tail points down, and a healthy tamed wolf's tail points up.

Fighting the Wolf

It's much smarter to never attack a wolf, because wolves remain hostile and they attack as a group. If, for some reason, you have inadvertently damaged a wolf and a pack is now after you, your best tactic is to escape. If you can, tunnel away and make sure to close off your tunnel's entrance! You'll need torches to light your way, of course. A hostile mob has a chance of despawning or disappearing from the game if it isn't within 32 blocks of a player for more than half a minute. They will definitely despawn if they are more than 128 blocks from a player. So tunnel away for at least 128 blocks before you come out.

CHAPTER 31
ZOMBIE

It's hard to make it through a night without seeing a zombie or a morning without seeing a zombie go up in flames. If you see one alight, strike it fast for a final death blow so you can get the XP.

Zombies are the most common hostile mob in Minecraft. In case you haven't noticed, the zombies look a bit like Steve with a turquoise T-shirt and blue pants. (There's a story in there somewhere!)

Some zombies spawn as zombie villagers, which have the same face as a villager, just green. And if a zombie attacks a villager, it will turn the villager into a zombie villager. There's also another type of zombie, the baby zombie, which you can read about in the baby zombie chapter.

The Husk is a variant of the zombie that wears brownish rags. It spawns only in deserts and is immune to the rays of the sun. Its attack will also give you the Hunger effect.

ZOMBIE STATS

Mob type: Hostile, Darkness

Health: 20

Attack Strength:

Easy – 2

Normal – 3

Hard – 4

Experience: 5

Drops: 0–2 rotten flesh, (more rarely) a carrot, iron ingot, potato, armor and weapons (if they holding them), a zombie head (if they are killed by a charged creeper)

Spawn: In Overworld in light levels of 7 or lower.

Sword Strikes to Kill:

Wood: 4

Stone: 4

Iron: 3

Gold: 4

Diamond: 3

Bow Strikes to Kill: 3

Fighting the Zombie

If you don't want to fight a zombie, just draw it into sunlight (if its day and you're not in a cave!). However, of all the common mobs, zombies are probably the easiest to defeat. They let you know pretty clearly when they're nearby with some good loud groans, and they move pretty slowly. If there's water between you and the zombie, it will take forever to get to you! And as you know, they will burn and die in sunlight (unless they are in water), making them a darkness-only pest.

A villager zombie burning up in the sun.

Zombies can spawn with armor, an iron shovel, or an iron sword. They can also pick up and wear armor, including mob heads dropped by a charged Creeper killing another zombie, skeleton, or Creeper. (This means you could find a zombie wearing a creeper head!) In any case, with armor, zombies become more difficult to kill, and while wearing a helmet they will not burn in the sun. Also, if you are playing on Hard mode, injuring one zombie will cause others to come help attack you.

A zombie with an enchanted shovel!

Use a bow and arrow to kill a zombie from a distance and you'll suffer no damage, as they can only attack you at close range. Wear a zombie head to sneak up on a zombie—you'll avoid detection until you're almost close enough to strike. Face to face, you should be able to knock a zombie out with your sword pretty easily; a sword enchanted with Knockback can also help.

CHAPTER 32

ZOMBIE PIGMAN

The zombie pigman is a very common mob in the Nether, but they are neutral. This means that if you ignore them, they will ignore you. And that is usually the best course of action. You can occasionally find them in the Overworld, as they can spawn near Nether portals. In the very rare chance that an Overworld pig is struck by lightning, it will turn into a zombie pigman, though without a sword.

ZOMBIE PIGMAN STATS

Mob Type: Neutral, Nether

Health: 20

Attack Strength:

Easy – 5

Normal – 8

Hard – 12

Experience: 5

Drops: 0–2 Rotten flesh, 0–1 gold nuggets, (more rarely) gold swords and gold ingots

Spawn: In the Nether at any light level and in the Overworld by a Nether portal or when lightning strikes close to a pig.

Sword Strikes to Kill*:

Wood: 4

Stone: 4

Iron: 3

Gold: 4

Diamond: 3

Bow Strikes to Kill*: 3

*The zombie pigman also has 2 armor points, which means you will need more strikes to kill it.

Fighting the Zombie Pigman

As with all neutral mobs, it's better to avoid fighting with zombie pigmen. Any zombie pigman within 67 blocks of an attacked pigman will be provoked and chase you. The only way to escape is to sprint (if you have a clear escape route), use a Potion of Swiftness, or ride away on a horse. You need to get 40 blocks away from the angered pigmen, fast, and give them 40 seconds to cool down. Leaving the Nether and coming back won't necessarily calm them down.

Pigmen always seem to want to get in your way, so be careful not to swing your axe or sword near them.

If you attack one zombie pigman, all the pigmen nearby will come in a horde to attack you.